Yours, etcetera

R. V. Bailey

Indigo Dreams Publishing

First Edition: Yours, etcetera
First published in Great Britain in 2019 by:
Indigo Dreams Publishing
24 Forest Houses
Halwill
Beaworthy
EX21 5UU

www.indigodreams.co.uk

ISBN 978-1-912876-24-2

British Library Cataloguing in Publication Data. A CIP record
for this book can be obtained from the British Library.

Designed and typeset in Palatino Linotype by Indigo Dreams.
Cover design by Ronnie Goodyer at Indigo Dreams
Cover painting Culverhay House by J. G. Collingwood
Printed and bound in Great Britain by 4edge Ltd
www.4edge.co.uk

Papers used by Indigo Dreams are recyclable products made
from wood grown in sustainable forests following the guidance
of the Forest Stewardship Council.

i.m. U A Fanthorpe (1929-2009)

Also by R. V. Bailey:

Course Work
Marking Time
Credentials
From Me To You (with U A Fanthorpe)
The Losing Game
A Scrappy Little Harvest

A Speaking Silence: Contemporary Quaker Poetry
(ed., with Stevie Krayer)
The Book of Love & Loss (ed., with June Hall)

CONTENTS

Yours, etcetera

A calling

She was a woman. A poor start in life, but you
Can't change that, and you soon learn. Even
As a child she was grown-up, and like a child she

Didn't count. There wasn't much money, so
There weren't many choices. She said *yes,*
All right, or else just *yes.* In a mixed class,

The teacher didn't ask her, anyway. Did he
Even know her name? The room was crammed,
And she was always at the back.

The last girl picked for a team, she wasn't
Good at friends. No one tried it on with her,
Or took what didn't happen further.

The telly made it clear it was her spots
(*Blemishes,* they called them). Or her breath?
She thinks it was her legs perhaps,

But didn't worry much. Being a woman's
All she knows – and what a woman does. She's
Not abused. She's fed. She's got a bed –

She's lucky. Some day someone will get
Something out of her. Things could be worse.

It's just a waste of time to write this verse?

A case of mistaken identity

That night, in the room with the Tudor
Window, we died. Both of us. You
In the proper way, tidily, resigned;
A cease of breath. Unhallowed and
Silent, unrecognised even by me,
I left, too.

Now ceremony surrounds you. At once
More real than you ever were, you
Are not here at all and this
Must be managed with tact, with
Office, with formal act. This is
What people do.

But – genuine ghost that I am –
I'm trapped in camouflage. I haunt
Invisibly; I'm taken for the one
I used to be – not some bit-part clot,
Baffled by the script of this black farce,
Who's lost the plot.

Being two people at once is perplexing,
Almost comic. Which face? the one
I've always worn – the one that's past?
Or the one I've only just been introduced to,
With its diffident grin? And this new, strange,
Confident cast?

OK, dear dead one – of course I know,
I hear what you're saying. *Just speak the lines, love.*
Just get on with the show.

A lot to ask

Each day's a sort of long dismay,
Learning afresh the lack of you:
I am a child who won't be told,
Can't be consoled.

Reading's my nearest friend:
Books holding the dark at bay
As they did for you, in the end.

Our loves expect so much of us:
We who are left behind –
A lot to ask, this daily going on,
Wanting more courage
Than we can find.

A mandarin

No. You can't have a scan.
You can have an X-ray
But it won't show anything.

Well, poor thing, it didn't.
Just some of the usual bones,
As it usually did.

It never noticed the
Interesting shape that
Looked like a mandarin.

You could hardly expect it to,
Since the doctor had made it clear
There was nothing there,

And he'd examined you.
What you need to do, he said,
Is just lose some weight.

Mandarins were obviously
Not on his mind that day.

Later it was too late
To do anything at all
About the inconvenient

Mandarin. Though you did,
Obediently, in the end,
Lose weight.

A visit

We talk about our journey,
About the new house (theirs),
About the cats (theirs, and ours).
Before the coffee's brewed we know
Something's up.

She doesn't look at him.
He talks about her daughter's husband.
She calls him by his name. In the garden,
We admire the roses, furtively
Squint at watches.

After a dutiful walk, we all sit down,
Drink tea, talk roses, cats. At last
We leave. And hear them as we go
Set about each other's wrongs
Hammer and tongs.

Airbnb (for Christmas 2018)

TripAdvisor gave the place two stars:
I'd have said one, at the most:
There wasn't much to eat;
The rooms were horribly draughty,
And none, of course, *en suite*.

The couple with the new–born baby
Were like us, relieved to be there:
They'd travelled all day, and again, like us,
Were only too glad to lie down in the hay,
And reluctant to make a fuss.

Years later we met the child, grown up:
Nice chap – though officially, we hear,
A bit off-message, so they gave him the chop.
It's odd that he seems alive, and near.

We never forgot it, that one-star night:
And – ah, the love – and the light!

Ambitions, including the split infinitive

To grow up. To go up, and not
Be sent down. To see the funny side,
Not to let the side down. To let up, to cheer on,

Not fall off. To not fall out.
To look forward, to sit near
The back. To be the first to leave.

To get out while the water's hot.
To arrive on the dot. To know
What to wear, what to say.

To rise above. To shut up.
To open, to give way.
To let off (but not let on).

To give up when it's time.
To tell jokes, to tell stories, but not
Tales. To know the rules,

And how to break the rules,
To make the rules (always
Including 'normally').

To understand, undertake, undergo;
To love, to care, to befriend.

To keep it all up to the end.

Autumn Term

The unmanageable summer is over,
Holiday postcards from Greece become more rare;
No longer do truck drivers strip to the waist,
And gardens of riverside pubs are empty.

Our friends have no more slides to show us
And promenaders have heard their last concerto,
Lollypop ladies terrorise highways;
Trees are browner, grass is greener, and

Hyacinth bulbs are back in Woolworths.
Next year's wallflowers stuff suburban gardens,
Hoses snake tidily in greenhouse corners,
While gangs of finches hi-jack hedgerows.

Almost we have reached the last Sunday-after-Trinity,
Can abandon the pretence that we enjoy summer
Since we never really feel equal to its demands.
Now the last of the swallows has gone, and now

We can comfortably settle to slog through winter
Which better suits our national disposition.

Because of you

It was because of you
I phoned the nurses to let them know
I'd made it home that night.

It was because of you
I smiled at people in the street
And made the undertaker laugh.

It was because of you
I washed my face and combed my hair
And put a clean shirt on.

It was because of you,
If you'd been here.
I did what you'd have done.

Beginning

Childhood was
Ringlets and a liberty bodice
The dog in the garden, and the tent blowing down.

Adolescence was
School and tennis
And problems too deep to be spoken of.

Growing up was
Finding somewhere to live,
Something to do, and making money last.

Finding you was
A blue sky a clean sheet a new start
The beginning of life.

Birthday Verses

Under the bed, the terrier,
Terrified; whose shuddering
Shook the bed-frame, echoed
The pulses of my mother as she
Pushed me into air, into

The thunderous air of the storm
That broke the waters of a ten-week
Drought. *It'll be a boy, I know.*
Another boy. My father, wisely,
Nowhere to be seen.

Your father was near, but alluded to
Puppies. The doctor took refuge
In jokes. *When they're little as this*
We usually throw them back,
And try again.

Such a fuss to arrive so fragile, and such
A long journey ahead. Such bustle to come
So bewildered. Was it the thunder that
Inverted me? And why were you
In such a hurry?

Neither of us properly fitted. Never fully-
Paid-up members of the human race.
Was it our stars, Horatio? What luck was it
That secretly plotted conjunction, that finally
Slotted us home?

Break-time at Cheltenham

She was slight, and greying. In her usual
Collar-and-tie and lab coat; lined face
Behind horn-rimmed glasses, trim hair
Short as a man's. Her name? Miss –

Whatsit. Just the lab assistant – so, like
The porter or the gardeners, her name
Not on the List of Staff.

I met her in the corridor, at break.

Her friend had died, I'd heard.
The only words I found:
I'm sorry about your friend.

The locked face. The words
She would have heard,
Among the milk-bottles and buns,
But not what I meant, a virtual stranger,

Trying to reach out. I scarcely understood
The words myself, not then, at break-time.

But it's break-time again. And I do, now.

Cherry tree for a Poet
Subhirtella autumnalis

In its contradictory way
Looks best in spring,
When its urgent petals
Can't wait for leaves.

For the rest of the year
Not much happens.
You relax beneath it,
Awaiting resurrection.

A happy companionship
Sharing the same soil.
Frail as the tree, you made
But modest shade; were good

At merging into background,
And deceptively quiet.
You settled in any soil,
And everyone liked your fruit.

But late, unlike your neighbour –
Ah, how you flowered!

Death in Staffordshire

When death came for my mother.
The nurse was in tears:
I couldn't hold the door, she said.

As if she could. All of it is
Part of the story, irresistible
As the day you were born,

The day you had to go to school,
The day war broke out.
The pages won't stop turning.
But nor can you close the book.

Desert Island Discs

I nearly drowned, getting here.
I suppose I should be glad
I'm not dead.

My choice of music? No song
Suggests itself. But already I've heard
The odd bird.

The melodies I know belong
To yesterday. And luxury? Ease?
You tease.

The Bible and Shakespeare?
I lost my reading glasses in the sea.
Those two are quite enough for me.

Will I survive? How will I pass
The time? What'll I do?
Haven't a clue.

But should you ever come this way,
And the paperwork's OK,
And you got the right publicity –

You might drop off the fee.

Destinations

The bus went as far as the Cemetery –
A point not lost on the jokey conductor.

The Cemetery Superintendent's son
Was Dennis; Una, tubercular daughter,

Lay dying at home. Outside in sunshine
Dennis and I found grave-stones

Useful wickets, until his sixes
Shattered the greenhouse.

Disciples in Gethsemane

A pretty poor lot, we think, curling up
And kipping at a time like this. On the edge of
What we've come to call The Easter Story.

They could have stayed awake. They didn't.
What did it mean? Not that they didn't love him.
Exhausted, abstracted, how could they know

How up against it he was, how it might
Have made a difference? He was, after all,
Human: afraid he'd get it wrong, afraid he'd fall,

As he did, weak as a kitten under the cross.
It was all about being human, as they were,
As we are, not the superhero
We'd like to think we'd be

If we'd been there.

Dream

Locked in the habits of a lifetime's
Hostile love, she and her mother.
In dream, I brought them together.

The others were there, a fading
Backdrop in the shade, insisting,
Wanting the group to be photographed.

And I? Confused, protesting
That they were against the light.
Her mother wary, untrusting, yet

Mellowed for a moment by tenderness –
By candle light, the party nearly over,
The coffee, even the brandy –

And I? Desperate to catch quickly
How it was with the two of them,
Their brief uprush of opened hearts

Quickly, before the dream had passed,
Quickly, to be sure that at last
It was all right, in the end.

Examination Board

(i.m. Nigel Dodd)

Midsummer, and windows are open.
The city traffic's restless argument
Rises through the hot afternoon,
And the tentative chimes of St Saviour's
Remind us, remind us.

Where we sit, the green baize cloth
Waits like a billiard table, but this is not a game.
The papers in front of us, flat and helpless,
Lie like the papers of the dead. Heat
Debilitates us, over-simplifies, frustrates

Impartiality; ignites assertions that command
STOP! to the lives, the hopes these white sheets
So desperately claim: last chance saloon, the last exams
– and who knows then what may come after.
Derision damns easily. Academics, after all, know best.

Heat makes us impatient, short-tempered,
Emphatic. 'Let's just get the damn job done:
...of *course* it won't do. Some of us have *standards*'.
Outside, the traffic sweats, like us, while
St Saviour's reminds us, reminds us, reminds us

Some of us have hearts.

Fame is the spur

Soon it will be forty-three years
Since we came here: years which meant,
For you, honours of all sorts, from
The Queen's Gold Medal downwards.

Since you left, I have kept the flame
Alight, so far as anyone so pedantic
Can, nourishing the archive,
Publishing The Work. I do my best

To emulate you, since it seemed to me
That's what you'd have wanted,
In the poetry line. I'm known
In the Co-op, and other local venues

Of cuisine or culture. But today, I realise,
I'm getting there. In the flower shop
She said *You talking about something
Somewhere? Didn't I see a poster?*

And in the car park, another chap,
Who said *I heard a poem of yours
The other day* – Fame at last, you see!

Something about bums on seats, it was,
He added. *I'm sorry. I'm afraid
That's the only line I can remember.*

Father's home

He was brave, generous,
Principled, hardworking;

Good-looking, carefully tailored.
He was genial, jokey. Other men

Liked him, liked his style.
A golfer, a cricketer, crisp

In white flannels, early on
The green, affable at the club.

At the end of the day, hearing
His car turn into the drive,

Hearts and minds stood to attention;
Assumed a difference. For he was

Right, and we were merely human.
His strict rule measured and found

Us wanting, like God in His
Less Christian moments.

Feckless

No gifts; no training
In anything at all useful:
Too ordinary to be good.

The wrath of God is nothing:
It's well-deserved, indeed, but
My own regrets are sharper,
More real than His thunderbolts,
And quite impossible to endure.

I hope He understands this. I feel
He could learn from me.

Garden

I made this garden for you.
No straight lines, you said,
On the phone from far away.

Sixty they'd paid you (a fortune)
For your first ever reading. So
We bought a vine, and a midget
Greenhouse.

Four fine limes were there, planted
Centuries ago. A bay tree, and
A plum tree. Two collared doves
Had built an improbable nest in the
Whitebeam.

Soon there were roses,
Poppies, potatoes, leeks,
And a beehive: presents from pals
Who knew far more than we did about
Gardens.

Randomly, generously, nature indulged
Our hapless horticulture; welcomed seeds
On the wind, refugees from who knows where,
None of which ever rooted or flowered in
Anything remotely resembling a
Straight line.

Getting on

I can't do two things at once any more.
I can't text when I'm shopping
In the co-op. I can't chat on the phone
In the street. I look both ways before
I cross, worry about falling over
Children and dogs. I'm always
Quite glad to get home.

You could tell he was getting on a bit:

How he watches the pavement anxiously –
It might suddenly rise, and trip him.
He who had gazed on horizons.

How he meets friends he's known for years:
He can't bring their names to mind till
After they've gone. Though he loves them.

He's left the list at home.
He'll have to come back later,
For the bread, if any's left.

It doesn't matter. None of it
Seems to matter much at all.
And that's a real blessing.

Getting there

For the lucky few, it may be only
A short hop: here one moment,
There the next. For all of us, the

Departure lounge, its alienating
Fixed grin, its purposeless sense
Of nowhere; its boarding pass imperatives
When your number's called.

For most of us, a long haul
From once to now, this side to that,
While night and day are in disarray
And time-zones swerve through stars.

Behind your eyelids demons dance.
Beside you restless figures stir,
Their indistinct intrusive purr
Disquieting, while far below,
Tides urge continents to and fro.

A long haul. Then all at once
The cabin crew is at the door.

And all at once the silent boatman's
Handing you ashore.

Grave

In the coffin, you look somehow wrong.
To help you seem yourself again
I put your glasses on.

As the closed casket sinks in earth
We hang around uncertain what to do
Now you are gone.

The ritual handful of soil I throw
Blows back in the breeze on my shoes
With the words I say.

The quiet stone will bear your name,
Poet. And mine, since I'll join you here
One day.

Happycat

It *was* like the cat. Or like the dog,
Watching humbly, ready
To be fed,

To be noticed, loved, played with,
Walked. Waiting till we took it
Seriously.

Happiness is such a modest thing –
Shy as a vanishing smile
While it's there.

Like politicians, of course we revere
All abstract nouns. But happiness invites
No statistics:

Too ordinary, too special; just
Taken for granted. Other interests
Interest us.

Happiness is the everyday dog,
Or the cat, or the milk bottle
On the step,

Till one day it's gone. Like the sun,
Slipped out, while no one was
Looking.

Now we can't find it. Is it under the bed?
Has it gone with the recycling? Is it locked
In the shed?

What was it like? I can't really remember.
It was furry; and snug. It lay on the rug –
It never *used* to roam –

    Might it hear if you whistled?

      Will it ever come home?

Hindsight

More insistent than the car ahead
Is the shadowing car on your tail,
Intent, it seems, on consummation.

In the mirror's backward glance
Fly the phantoms of the past,
Isadora's scarf – diaphanous, deadly.

This milk was spilt too long ago; its
Soured magic can't be drunk today.

So don't look back. Drive on.
Drive fast away.

If you weren't here

If you weren't here I'd hate going out
To smell cold air and watch clouds and
Consider things in woods;

Or to buy wine and garlic and mushrooms
Or a selection of appropriate tins of cat food
For our highly discriminating cat.

I wouldn't want to go out to coffee
Or tea or supper with anyone at all.
I wouldn't want to drive the car,

Even to exceptionally agreeable places such
As Scotland or Ireland or Wales (let alone
To take my teeth to the dentist).

I wouldn't look forward to the heady drama
Of the North Circular, or Hyde Park Corner;
Or the frisson of particularly challenging

Situations on the M25. I'd hate to go to plays.
I wouldn't want to cheer up folks in hospitals or in
Old folks' homes. I wouldn't want to walk the dog

Or go to town, to post the letters or pay the bills,
Or to buy even a highly desirable book. I wouldn't
Want to go anywhere, as a matter of fact,

If you weren't here to come home to.

If you were here

I'm as cheerful as anyone could be,
Without you. Proof-reading poems,
Writing; chasing e-mails and letters. But

..... if you were here

Respectfully the garden waits to help; the shed
Is trying to catch my eye; the car would be obliged...
Your not being here fills the house. And sunshine

Leaks from the grass, brightness from the brave
Untidy poppies you liked so much.
If you were here, I'd notice the impetuous

Excesses of May-time. I'd understand
What the blackbird is trying to tell me. I'd be
Tinkering about in the garden shed.

..... if you were here

Mind you, I'm so sorry for myself without you
You'd be thoroughly ashamed of me

.... if you *were* here.

In the passenger seat

I know. Yes: I should be
Grateful. Should be
At peace, within, wherever,
Heaven, and so on. Yes, I know.

> But Lord, I'm not. To me
> *This* world's what's what:
> Even here, in the fearful dark,
> As landscape rushes past
> The swerving car, here's
> My home. The only tongue I speak.

How should I understand
What's called the afterlife? How bear
The novelty of heaven, if that is where –
Quite apart what may have to take place
En route there?

> I'm deep in *things,* Lord, *here* – breakfast time,
> Spring, putting the milk-bottles out,
> Letting the cat in –
> Can't just leave, step off. Please, not yet,

Lord – I'd really like to feel Your hand was on the wheel.
Meanwhile I clutch the map,
Await my fate.

I'm sorry

Never explain, never apologise ~ Disraeli

It comes of course as part of the deal,
With certain vocations. Doctors,
Lawyers would diminish; would lose

Their clients' confidence: we need their ichor
Of omniscience. Without it, litigation, loss of trade – who
Knows what may follow? Even Prime Ministers

Have found themselves redundant.
Yet think of it: all those unused apologies,
Piling up over the years – what colossal

Stamina it must take to sustain a whole lifetime
Of never saying sorry. In the end, I suppose,
Even the possibility dies, for lack of exercise.

But just consider: suppose you took that key
To the big black lock, and turned it.

What would happen then? Appalled
Silence – the shock of the new? Scorn, perhaps?
Perhaps a stammered attempt at forgiveness –

And heaven only knows how you'd even begin
To manage that.

Last rights

Well-attended, decorous, the funeral
In the Crematorium Chapel. They were
Proud of her, her clever doctor brother,
His wife, their children's clever aunt:
Her school career; her Oxford days.
Her scholarship (though no one used
The word *aegrotat*).

No one mentioned the dark, the despair,
The loneliness, or the hospital.

She took her erudition back to the school
Who'd taught her; passed on her own
High notions of sound learning – could
Quote by the yard the English poets,
And always aptly.

Her clever doctor brother led the service.
We all admired her brilliance that reflected
So creditably on them all, on all of us.

A final hymn. And that was it.

No one had even mentioned
Her kindness. Her courage.
Or her wit.

To those of us who'd known Miss Ball
She wasn't there at all.

Leavings

Other people leave dogs to be found a home for,
Cats who'll not settle, furniture no one wants.
Some leave homes, and children. Even money.

You've left only yourself, disguised as poems.
And there's more of you now than I ever
Suspected, and more mysteriously:

Paper scraps with words, teasing messages
That blow like fragments from the Sybil's cave.
Who could collate such imaginative flair?

I'd like to think you've left yourself in careful
Hands but I'm clumsy, and the genie's fled the
Bottle – your enchantment's in the air.

You who felt you never fitted
Now belong everywhere.

Lend me your ears: the translator speaks

Oh yes, mine are nice enough
And they do their job without
Complaining. They've never
Been much trouble, and they aren't
Now. It's just that I want to hear

What *you* hear; want to catch
The timbre, the scent of the voices
That speak in a language I don't speak,
Have only learnt. I want to hear the
Things no one would think
Of telling me. Not just the words.

Long haul

Lovers can manage it easily
Sliding with confidence into
Each other's topography.

Old hands fold themselves
Into laptops and films,
Fall asleep as if in bed.

We cross oceans; continents
Slide impassively beneath us,
Making no demands, while

Shackled by propinquity
My neighbour and I move
Taut and tentative as suspects.

His mahogany arm lies
Unhappily on mine, his warm
Thigh is a hostile radiator.

Fourteen hours of unwilling
Intimacy lie ahead: a lifetime's
Sentence, wordless, silent, since

Language is unshared. Even
Our well-intentioned gestures
Fall to the floor like dead birds.

O to be a lover. Or to be
In business-class. Or to be
Anywhere... just to be alone.

Love, etcetera

I'm not good at writing letters.
There's always so much to say, and
So many words. A protracted education,
A long and undistinguished life,
A thesaurus, a dictionary: all these
Unfitted me for what I want to say.

None of it helps, when words
Matter so much, have such dignity,
Such integrity, can so easily
Burst into flames. For instance,

There is love. But there is also, you see,
Etcetera – everything else. Such a lot of it,
And all of it matters – war, and rivers,
Lunacy and loneliness, bears and woodlice,
The blackbird in the evening
And the smell of hope –

Let's not even mention adjectives.

I am too shy to use that big
Four-letter word. And yet, and yet –
Haphazardly, absurdly,
Most sincerely I remain

Yours,

        etcetera.

Made to measure

Mouths, for instance:
Invented for all the nicest things.
Eating, talking, singing, smiling;
Kisses.

Noses? For the smell of the sea,
For blowing after crying, or
Importantly, when you can't think
What to say.

Ears let you listen to music,
Gossip, the roar of the lion and the beat
Of the heart, the watch's tick and
The baby's cry.

You need your knees
For scrubbing the floor, for picking
Daisies, for apologising
To God.

And eyes are the way the world
Gets to you, with its squalor,
Its loveliness, all its offerings of
Possibility.

Making jam

A mouse there was. Maybe
More than one. Two mice
Could raise a family

In the piano. Cat and dog
Opened a scornful eye:
Mice quite beneath them.

Mouse-trap? Couldn't face
Setting it. Another trap,
Plastic, humane? OK.

Daintily the mouse took cheese,
Didn't spring the trap. What
Good table-manners.

More cheese: a grateful
Mouse. The piano watched,
Anxiously.

The pet-shop's Fortnum-
and-Mason's *Mouse Treats* –
Over-priced; sticky – but irresistible.

Next day, let her go,
All eyes and whiskers, in
The leafy churchyard.

But – whoops! Door's slammed shut
And I've got no key...

Inside, on the hob, the jam's boiled dry.
But the mouse is free.

Minefield

My father was an unexploded bomb.
My mother's motto, *peace at any price,*
Modified, did not eliminate, the risk.

My strategy, mutinous silence, only
Intensified wrath: growls, mutters,
Like thunder in the offing.

Sometimes there was singing. Then
Customary wariness might cautiously
(umbrellas at the ready) be shed.

Such welcome times were not
To be relied on. I had no cover
Against his scorn, and he no words

For me. On a good day, cricket
Might be conversation territory; though
Not politics, neighbours, or the news.

What would I say to you now,
Old man? Nothing, probably.

I can still hear the ticking.

Mr Findlay

You could call me a bit of a bodger, really,
He said, when first we met.
A Barnardo's boy, he became
The shoulder we cried on
When things went wrong, and

Quite a lot of things went wrong,
As they do, when you first move house.
There was nothing, it seemed, that he
Couldn't handle: paint the ceilings?
Move the hand-basin? Fix that window

We can't open? *How about Monday?*
A philosopher, he'd interpret everything,
Satisfyingly, in detail, at considerable length,
Over coffee. I, meanwhile, might do
A spot of woodwork, paint a picture,

Have a bash at Bach and Beethoven
When time allowed. And you began life as a poet.
Mr Findlay was paid; unqualified, you and I
Mere threadbare apprentices in a gig economy.

Yet we were all of us bodgers,
Then and now: serious amateurs,
Practising the mystery. Learning how to be
Properly professionally human.

My French Piece
(for J S Bach)

She is fickle. She waits for me to come,
And then won't play. My timing
Isn't all it should be. There are days

When nothing I can do pleases her
And no one would want to hear
The conversation between us.

That she is tricky is generally agreed
By those who know her. They also agree
That she is lovely beyond words.

She's been around for a long time.
You need to know harpsichord
To understand her properly, and

Not many of us know that. But today
She is coming to meet me. Today
She plays into my hands.

Nature Poem

Nature sits there
All the time
Waiting to be looked at
Exclaimed over
Written about

Ready to comply with,
Or illustrate, as metaphor,
Our everyday concerns.

Wordsworth noticed her
Without being told; and
Sister Dorothy supplied
Some of the best words.
A lot of walking was done.

I'm glad we have the National Trust.
Now we don't need to worry about
Noticing and saying the right things
We can just have tea
And buy the postcards.

Nightmare

At the end of the day
When all's said and done,
The last drop drunk,
The last line writ,
And the last lap run

The worst
Comes to the worst.

Philosophy, lifetime crony,
Turns out to be junk;
Does a bunk.

You're at the funeral
You're about to speak:
But the words in your pocket
Are written in Greek....

You're standing in the pulpit
But you've missed your cue
The poor fellow's dead:
There's nothing you can do

      Till you waken – shaken,
      Shaken –

          At home. In bed.

Not serious

She was skilled at crosswords
Completed them every day, always
Got them right, even the prize ones,

Which she never sent in. He didn't,
As a rule, do crosswords, having less
Time, but sometimes he wrote poems,

Which he never sent in. Naturally
Neither of them ever came near
To winning a prize. Not serious?

No: for them, it was the pleasure
Of the game, not the fame. One day
Some grubby, folded, filled-in

Crossword, keeping someone's place,
May slip out of a book; or maybe
A bit of scribbled verse remain.

Who did this book belong to? you ask.
Oh – some poet fellow. I forget his name.

Occupation

Doctor? Not what you think, if you
Think at all. No blood or bandages.
(Something to do with hearts...?)

To mention *Writer* as an alternative,
Suggests celebrity idleness. Yet the form
(There is always a form) requires

Some indication of what I get up to
In the usual working hours. *Poet*'s
A questionable title: furtive, even:

A kind of burglary suggests itself.
Decidedly a suspect calling – a
There and not-there sort of thing:

Nothing you'd notice. Maybe even
A body-snatcher (almost respectable, in
Its time), digging up what was perhaps

Better left buried. A picker-up of trifles;
Things left idly lying about. A thief –
Of thoughts, words, hopes, that

Properly belong to others, though it's I
Who overhear them. Quite honestly

I've still no idea what's the right term
To put on the form.

Old soldier

Nothing extenuate,
Nor set down aught in malice.
(Othello V Scene II, 311)

In the end, an unmarked grave.
Your wife too done in to care,
And the rest of us indifferent
To where your ashes are.

You gave your kids a start in life
More promising than your own.
None of us got love right. I'd say
The blame's not yours alone.

On your birthday, yet again

There's not a lot just one can do
But tonight I drink this single malt for you:
You'd have joined me here today
If we'd had our way.

It's never too late to say hurrah
For all the things you were –
And – I'm pretty certain –
In some sense somewhere probably
Still are.

That seditious chuckle;
Your double (whoops) –
Jointed-ness; your tolerance

Of me. Your resolutions.
(Your magical puddings.)
Your circumlocutions.

All the things you'd said and done,
All those things you never forgot –

But hey, I shouldn't go on:

To list these festive quiddities won't do:
I'd take all too readily to the bottle
If I were to celebrate everything
About you.

Oncologist
(for Dr Candish)

You'd had to get there by wheelchair.

Outside, sunshine. Inside, it was
The sort of waiting-room where
Everyone already knew the score:

Only whispers here; no proper chat.
Too many patients, too few consulting-rooms:
Ours was a tiny store-room, with a bed,

But nowhere to sit. He dropped to his knees
Beside your chair, beside you. Gently, he
Told us what we already knew. And said

He'd see you again before long. (We
Privately thought that by then you'd be dead.)

Nothing had changed, as we left. The hushed
Grey patients waited. Outside, the sun was still bright,
But this time we noticed it. Because of the man

On his knees close beside you that day,
Our frightening world seemed suddenly
Somehow manageable; somehow almost
Okay.

Part-time
(for Dr Fowler)

'Only a part-time GP', we'd been told,
The woman we'd turned to.
As though she didn't count.

She made more than a part-time difference
For us. Almost every morning, just
To see how things were. Easy as a friend,

Sitting by the sofa where (horizontal but
Courteous as ever) you lay, she'd listen.
Let you talk, frail, helpless, apprehensive,

Day by day, as if what you spoke of
Was new – was even interesting – to her,
Who must have heard it all before.

She spoke of the future as if there was a future,
As if there were still things that would help,
That would make it easier for you, lying

On the ordinary sofa, in morning sunshine,
In the kind of urgent solitude only the dying
Know. Perhaps I thanked her properly,

When it was over. I hope I did. I hope she knew
What a difference her daily visits made for you.

Photograph

Good-looking young man in a blazer,
By a Nottinghamshire tree, near the Trent.

Nothing had happened to him then,
Except my mother, and their happiness,
Not long before they wed. All his life,
In that day's sunshine, lay before him.

Nothing there that day to suggest
The flooding tide of another river, war,
Or of what he felt, and saw; or how the sunshine
Faded. After, he was never a man for words.
No words, in any case, would do.

He never spoke of the dark that swallowed him
Near Bullecourt, that swallowed the sun
For ever. That took him into a night
That never left him: that tarnished, in time,
Wife, family, children; that happiness by the Trent.

A long life. A decent honest life; principled,
Successful, always good-looking. A handful only
At his funeral, and no one knows exactly
Where his ashes are, or who purloined
His medals. No one can guess

How different it all might have been
If those years had never happened
Before nineteen eighteen.

Saying nothing to Staff-Nurse

(i.m. Vera Williams)

When I went to London, I left my heart
In Cambridge. Gently, my heart
Accepted me, loved me back,
As far as a woman could.

It was the fifties, and so of course
Nothing was said. Only shy love,
Decorous, acceptable. A weekend
At Westgate, where her parents lived.

Of course I let her down: a new job,
A new place, another she, as gentle,
As generous. With whom, again,
Nothing at all was said.

Scar tissue

— I'm sorry sir. That's not enough.

Lank and grey, he stood, hesitantly
Pushing over the counter a scatter of coins,
In front of her at the grocer's.

Sorry, he said. And turned away.
She could, that day, have made a difference.
It wasn't a large sum, and she had enough.

Could we have a dog? Half a century ago
The boy wanted a dog. *No, I can't
Cope with a dog,* she said, *there's a war on.*

And so the boy went off to fight,
Was wounded, came home;
Left for Australia, for life.

Such moments stay, vivid as scars:
The times she could have said yes
To the boy, or when, preoccupied

In the grocer's shop, she didn't think
To open her purse. A lifetime between
Then and now, for her, at ninety-five.

The great glad moments fade; are gone.
There's still the dog, the poor man in the shop,
And what she could have done.

Self's the man

His wife was elegant, kind: talented,
A credit to him. He could take her anywhere.

Indeed, though no one said so, we all thought
The better of him that he sported such a wife.

But she was ill, he said. Not glamorously ill, and
Not heroic: no blood or bandages. Just

Un-diagnosedly ill. That night,
We talked about her symptoms – and his plight.

Inconvenient, in a way, to have a wife like this:
A fellow didn't know, from day to day,

Where he was with her. Should he leave?
Divorce? What did I think? He thought he might.

Nothing I said seemed any use. Then *After all,*
He said, as we were in the hall, *I ask myself*

What's in it for me? Not just a whim –
That seemed the clinching argument, for him.

This conversation came to me years later
When both his subsequent wives proved traitor.

Semi

With three narrow beds,
A chest of drawers, two desks,
Several thousand books
And a piano, we moved in.

Armchairs had to lurk alone
In the shed, whose corrugated roof
Just about kept the rain out.
To stop the damp from rising

We laid bricks, filched from
Abandoned building sites.
Over the sink, we put up a light, so
We could see to do the washing up.

As for the name of our brave estate,
Hanging on a mountain by Merthyr,
No one even attempted to spell –
Let alone pronounce it.

Not quite the leafy suburbs. I don't
Recall trees. But sheep tucked into all
Our gardens at midnight. Quite soon,
A damp stray kitten moved in.

Our luxury was a telephone box
Round the corner. Neighbours called
The place *God's Own Country. Wales,
The Land of Song*. Did we sing?

You bet we did.

Six dogs

His tiny bristly dog trots confidently ahead.
I don't look down, as they approach; I know
His master will be wearing slippers.

Large, elderly, black, rheumaticky:
He cautiously wags his tail. At the other end
Of his lead, grizzled, complaining, rheumaticky,
His master doesn't smile.

She hurls herself at my feet, smiling,
Curls in a ball to offer her tummy for tickling.
We chat, her owners and I. They know
If I could, I'd steal their dog.

At last this dog's grown up. Together, for years
They've rambled the woods. Together remarked
Aconites, and deer. They've watched the fox.
Better by far than shopping with the wife, he says.

Cheerful adolescent, he hurtles down the hill as
I brace my knees to meet him. He grins at me, wants me
To throw a stick. His master's good for a chat: he wants
Me to share his outrage. There's always something
To have strong views about.

This whippety creature's aloof; his mind's elsewhere.
His master's mind's in the clouds; he'd like to be there.
His wife is on earth, dying. Neither man nor dog
Can do more for her. Together they need to escape
Briefly, sadly, into the empty afternoon air.

Small print

Arrival: the parents' hopes,
Midwife's attention,
The general whoopee
That attend delivery –
The postman's load
After *The Times* told all.

What happens later?
Anyone's guess: from
Potty training to words,

Meanings, other people;
The game of consequences
That isn't a game at all.

The long road of learning,
From knowing nothing to
Understanding far too much.

And oh, with luck,
First-footing Love,
Sharp, undeniable,
Offering and requiring
Nothing less than all,
And everything that follows.

Departure is
Feet first, last post:
How or when only
Small print in *The Times*.

The language of the past
Is ruthless. It offers
No second chances.

Susceptible

– to hay fever, idleness and marmalade,
I don't find it hard to turn my back
On shopping, lying on the beach, or work.

As far as people are concerned
(and they are right to be concerned)
I can't resist the good. And if the good

Are lovely, why, so much the better,
Though beauty's not essential. If
They like to laugh, a low and subversive

Chuckle will readily light my flame.
And if they are clever as well,
Consider me lost.

Syllabics on giving a poetry reading

On leaving: the ritual
Anxious pacing of loved space,
Locks, lights, curtains.

Driving: and the homesick tug
Of what's behind; of unknown
Perils ahead.

Being there, and settling in:
Unpacking, waiting, changing:
Another self.

At last all's over. Glad rags
Gladly cast aside, and now
A whisky waits.

Tea next morning, bags packed,
Sun-streaked roads: the jubilant
Journeying home.

Talking, afterwards

What can I do for you now?
  Feed the birds, wind the clock.
What can I give you?
  There is nothing I lack.

How can I please you now,
You so quick to delight?
  I was always pleased by you
  (And I was always right).

What can I say to make you laugh?
What subversive anecdote?
  I want to hear it all one day.
  Don't worry: I'll wait.

Teachers in Wartime
(i.m. Charles Russell)

They were too old for the army.
Teaching was a reserved occupation;
They couldn't get away.

Morgan Hall, whose name suggested
A National Trust destination, taught Art;
Treated us to tea in his country house.
All my paintings looked convincing,
Since Morgan always finished them off.

George Worsley, deputy Head, was
Decidedly donnish: we'd hide from him
When it was French, in some wrong room, to see
How long it took for him to find us.

Madame Louet's husband (we didn't ask)
Was away in France somewhere, at war,
Fighting more serious foes than we were.

Len Morrow, invalided out of the RAF,
Still had malaria. Tall, handsome in his
Officer's British Warm, he'd be waiting
Gaunt and shaking at the bus stop
Hours before school was over.

Mr Williams, too: parachuted from
The Front – most patient mathematician;
Having settled the rest, he'd turn to me, and
Slowly explain everything all over again.

Miss While? Tried very hard to teach me History.
A good essay, long, well written. Except
You haven't included a single fact.

Charles Russell: the lively magician
Who'd survived the Burma railway:
Whose hair was prematurely white.

See what I've got for you today, he'd say,
Springing into the early room: *I want to know*
Exactly what you think about the Four Quartets...

Arguing about Eliot – about everything
For the rest of our lives – it was how we'd be.
He knew about escaping. He'd set us free:

The dreamer's complaint

Always a double act, as things were. Now
It's only at night that you come.

But you've not changed at all and so
It feels, when you do, like home.

To see you by day would be good
But I know how you're placed. I daresay

You'd come like a shot if you could –
That was always your way.

Earthbound I wait, your obstinate lover;
While you are on night-shift for ever,

Still haunted by history, and words, and war,
And people and rivers. And how things are.

The Idea of a University
(With apologies to John Henry Newman)

Doctorates descend like petals in a wind
On these graduates. Such tinsel titles,
Once the pinnacles of a life-long ascent
Into the rarefied air of distinction, now
Commonplace. Yet mere Bachelors of Arts
Still can't spell, despite so many
Improvidently awarded Firsts.

Humanity, the thing we all share,
Gets lost in this forest of excess.
Soon babies will arrive not with
Silver spoons in their mouths,
But with rabbit tippets on their
Swaddling-clothes and an honours-
Board of ready-gilded exclamations.

Theses – *Shakespeare's use of the semi-colon*
In the later history plays – peer-reviewed
Papers, cited, post-modern, accredited –
Won't pay the milkman; nor will densest prose
Empower a plumber when you need him most.

I've never met a single semiotic that could
Deconstruct an unintelligible dishwasher.

The keys of the kingdom

Like next-door neighbours we hold the keys
Of the kingdom for each other. And quietly
When they went, they slipped their signatures
Through our letter-box, just in case.
I think of my father (though we didn't get on),
And pay bills by return. Haunted by mother,
Who took heartbreak on the chin and made a joke
Of it, I mock my own absurdity.
And you – ah you, who are always there –
Your magic makes me whole. Makes me
Forget myself altogether.
Ghosts have no sense of decorum.
Who's to say where it will end?

The end of April

It was the end of April,
as migrant birds crossed deserts
and an English sky at its best
to friendly crevices in ancient barns
and familiar homely nests.

It was the end of April,
as Chaucer's travellers got
their Canterbury gear together
for horseback days and godliness
and gossip and better weather.

Perversely you considered
spring over-rated, showy.
So you left at the end of April
without timetables or luggage:
stepping into bird-space and travellers' joy

The live thing

Is putting up a pheasant on the hill,
Or asleep in front of the fire,
Or dreaming of lettuce in its hutch.

Only later you think
I wish I'd kept that photograph.
Why did I burn those letters?

No letter, dog-lead, derelict hutch, though each
A link in the chain, is enough:

The past catches fire from these embers
But fingers burn. It won't do.

It's the living, the living, we want. To love them
Here on the hill, at our side, in the hutch;
Hand in that warm other hand,

While they're alive.

The novelist's socks

(for Mark Pasco)

Are, much of the time, moist
With the kind of dewy sensibility
It takes to be a writer. Privy to moments
Of toe-clenching shame, as well as
Breathless adulation, they
Are alert to the scent of clay.

That they don't always match
Is, naturally, a delicate signal
Of genius. That they seldom find
Themselves together in the laundry basket
An indication of a similarly
Erudite absence of mind.

You must not take these aberrations
Seriously. They denote inspiration,
Are responsive to climatic conditions
Prevailing with their owner: warm front,
Occluded, the shipping forecast's litanies,
His Beaufort Scale from Calm to Storm.

Plot, counter-plot and character weave
Amid the cumulus. He is Creator, Nemesis,
Designer of dynasties. Despair and suicide
Infect his keyboard hands. And yet
Famously his halcyon touch can magic
A fretful insomniac to sleep. Not so

His own intractable weather. His wife
Has long ago escaped the plot. No
Tailored draft can now recover her, nor
Weave his children from their wilderness.
The layabout sea watches him at his desk,
Does nothing to help. A cloud-
capped palace awaits his attention.
His toes curl at the prospect of coffee.

The poet's accomplice describes what happens

First, there's waiting, in the dark, in the wings.
Technicians move avidly, knowing their job.
Interlopers, here for one night only, we're
Apprehensive.

Then on stage. The audience knows how to behave:
Hopeful and ready to respond, they listen,
They sigh, or chuckle, or applaud. Or not.
No problems here.

Afterwards, I'm hanging about, while you're
Hard at it, talking, listening, signing books,
Coffee at your elbow long gone cold; the porter
Rattling his keys.

Lights out now, and the crowd gone. The porter
Locked up years ago. I'm still here, hanging about,
Waiting in the wings. Ready to join you, when it's
Time to go home.

The ragged hem

The ragged hem, the finger-nail. The give-away,
More trustworthy than talk. Dropped

Conversational stitches. The little words,
Common, that no one notices; particular,

That carry so much weight. Though you'd never
Weigh them. Nor fit them in a box, yes or no.

Tail of a sentence no one's any longer
Listening to. What's real leaves clues,

Like finger-prints. Where to look, how to see:
Imagination tidying, making manageable
A world that can't be understood.

(Not accountants' currency,
Correct, self-important;
Meaningless.)

Watch. Look. Listen. It's all there, the truth.

Trust me, I'm a doctor

Your name is Doctor:
I may call you God.

My name is Patient:
I have no other name.

You ask what *seems*
To be the matter?

My suspect symptoms
Fail to convince even me.

I have no words. But you
Supported by technology,

Have no such doubts.
Guilty of pain, of failure,

I waste your sacred time,
Your lofty erudition. I must

Pull myself together, lose
Some weight. Stand up tall.

Unfortunately here
I carry no weight at all.

Turning the clocks back

Not back to unmanageable teens,
Sunny twenties – the well-deserved
Pratfalls of youth. Just, say,

Before the letter came; before the accident,
The holiday. When what was said
Was still unsaid, still time to get it right...

Ah! but that great fixer Time won't
Play the game. Its modes are History
And Now. Turn away.

Chuck the censorious clock. Another day
With unimagined plenty's
On the way.

Walking in the woods

Not what you'd call a brisk walk:
More a policeman's tread, checking
– as they used to do – that the town's
In place at midnight.

Here, with no one but squirrels, trees, a fox
Or two, and Gloucestershire birds
Providing the sound-track, I learnt
How to be alone.

(I also learnt to hate. I won't describe that –
Though a rigmarole of silent maledictions
Muffled the birds, almost obliterated the
Innocent wildlife.)

Ten years later, here we are again. I've learnt
Friendship with solitude, finding it fitting,
Steady, a sound vocation. I've settled gratefully
Into its mild cell.

I'm not going to tell you how much harder
The other thing's to deal with. But love
Is other. Absolute, non-negotiable, it
Will, in the end, win.

What the tortoise said

It's a good day for the race, my father said.
– *What race? I didn't know there was a race today.*
It never failed. *The human race,* he said.

The tortoise wasn't sure.
Did it apply to him? He wasn't
Human. Which race, and who

Was expected to run? and where?
What was the prize? He didn't know
What the rules of entry were.

Everyone else, he thought, had it straight.
He was too shy to ask. All he could do
Was wait

Till Aesop came. Then it was clear:
Slow and steady was his job. And the hare?
Just a flash,

A hundred-yards-dash.
Because of his fabled lumbering pace,
She finished first. There was no disgrace –

He'd take his time.
He'd get there just the same.

Who won the prize?
The question's quite absurd:
Apart from Aesop, nobody cared.

Words to conjure with

It's OK – you don't have to call yourself a Christian.
That's a word where too many difficult relations
Are all too ready to drop in, some of whom
You really wouldn't want to meet for a coffee
However many custard tarts were on offer.

'Quaker' has what you might call (that's to say,
If you were a sociologist) a more respectable
Line in social capital. But beware: you might
Find yourself in over the ears, with altogether
Too much to live up to.

Catholic? A whiff of incense, a hint of
Mystery, aristocracy, priest holes and burning
At the stake. Though you'd like to think
Of yourself as being forgiven, the idea of
Confession's enough to put anyone off.

In the end, maybe all of these will do:
Just leave out the capital letters, or better still
Don't even mention any of the words. Lie low,
Remember what you already know
About being Christian. And just get on with it.

Indigo Dreams Publishing Ltd
24, Forest Houses
Cookworthy Moor
Halwill
Beaworthy
Devon
EX21 5UU
www.indigodreams.co.uk